GW00854555

The Highlands & Islands of Scotland in Colour

Text by JENNY CARTER

Photographs by DENNIS HARDLEY

B. T. BATSFORD LTD · LONDON

Text © Jenny Carter 1983
Photographs © Dennis Hardley 1983

First published 1983

All rights reserved. No part of this publication may
be reproduced, in any form or by any means,
without permission from the Publisher

ISBN 0 7134 3825 8

Typeset by Typewise Limited, Wembley, Middlesex
and printed in Hong Kong
for the publishers
B. T. Batsford Ltd.
4 Fitzhardinge Street
London W1H 0AH

Contents

The photographs on pages 44-47 are reproduced by permission of the Scottish Tourist Board

The Highlands

The Laggan Dam in full
flood, Inverness-shire

reign (1034-58) was on the whole peaceful, and Queen Gruoch (Lady MacBeth) was queen in her own right.

North of Cawdor mediaeval history and fortifications give way to the sad story of eighteenth-century Jacobitism, and the happier consequence of a fine specimen of military architecture. Near Ardersier, once a tiny village dependent on the nearby fort, and now developed as a base for the construction of steel production platforms for the thriving North Sea oil industry, stands the imposing Fort George. After the Rising of 1715, General Wade, under command to impose military control over the unruly Highland clans, established a chain of forts across the Great Glen – Fort William on the west coast, Fort Augustus at the western end of Loch Ness, and Fort George on Castle Hill in Inverness. In 1746, 20 years after it was built, Fort George was seized by the Jacobites and blown up. Two years later, Scotland's great architect, Robert Adam, was commissioned to replace it, and building commenced near Ardersier; the present fortification, still garrisoned, was the result.

On Culloden Moor was fought the last battle to be waged in the United Kingdom. In truth, it was less a battle than a massacre. On 16 April 1746 Prince Charles Edward Stuart, in a final bid to establish his claim to the throne, gathered his followers to meet the forces of the Hanoverian government under the command of the Duke of Cumberland. The battle was as brief as it was bloody. In 40 minutes, 1,200 Highlanders were slaughtered, and a romantic dream shattered. Today a cairn stands as memorial to the event, and headstones commemorate the clansmen who fought and died there. At Old Leanach Cottage, round which the battle raged, the National Trust for Scotland has a small museum and audio-visual exhibition.

Glen More Albin, the 'Great Glen' as it is more commonly known, traverses Scotland for 60 miles from Fort William in the south-west to Inverness in the north-east. This spectacular geological fault divides Scotland in two, and a series of lochs stretch along its length, linked now by the Caledonian Canal, a major waterway that obviates the necessity of circumnavigating the turbulent waters round Cape Wrath in the north of the Scottish mainland.

Of the lochs that lie along the Great Glen, Loch Ness is by far the largest, and also the most notorious. The waters of the loch remain uncharted; undoubtedly deeper in many places than the 700 feet on record, the murky waters, contorted fissures, and an unknown depth of silt on the loch bottom make more accurate charts impossible. Many visitors will find its long vistas and tree-shaded shoreline the main attractions of the loch. To some its importance will be as the grave of John Cobb, who died here in his attempt to break the world water speed record in 1952. And many are the sailors who will merely enjoy cruising at leisure along the 24-mile stretch of water. But for the vast majority Loch Ness has become the focus of a sport that began as recently as 1932 – 'Nessie-hunting'. In 1932 a local man reported sighting a strange creature rearing up from the waters of the loch; others were quick to add further reports of such sightings of the water monster. 'Nessie', as she was dubbed, rapidly became a celebrity. In recent years serious scientists have attempted to verify the existence of a creature or creatures in the loch, but to date no acceptable proof has been offered to a still sceptical public. Nevertheless 'Nessie' remains a major attraction, and motorists, particularly on the main A82 road that runs close to the loch, should pay

particular attention to the road, and not to the loch, when driving.

Loch Ness, in fact, offers many other attractions besides elusive water creatures. Amid the hills that flank the south-eastern shores are scattered several pretty lochs – not so small either, except in comparison with their massive near neighbour: Loch Duntelchaig, Loch Ruthven, Loch Ashie and Loch Mhor. Real Highland lochs these, not protected round and about with shady trees and lavish vegetation, but lying open to the bare moorland. Yet the reflections of sky and hill on a bright summer's day, the rare glimpse, perhaps, of a graceful Slavonian grebe paddling along with her chicks on her back, and the remarkable quiet of this area are attraction enough to those who value solitude and the sights and sounds of the countryside.

When the road returns to Farigaig Forest, the scene becomes busier, for this is a major Forestry Commission site, and besides all the everyday business of the Commission, a well laid-out nature trail running among the conifers and broadleaves attracts many visitors. Nearby the Falls of Foyers cascades in two great bounds down an impressive 120 feet into the ever receptive waters of Loch Ness.

Fort Augustus at the south-western tip of the Loch was one of the chain of forts established by General Wade. Built in 1730, it was named after William Augustus, Duke of Cumberland. It was blown up by the Jacobites in 1746, but re-built and regarrisoned until the Crimean War. Only one wall of the Fort still stands. In 1867 the lands were sold to Lord Lovat, who gave them to the Benedictine Order which built an abbey there; the school now here is run by Benedictine monks.

The major landmark on Loch Ness is Urquhart Castle. Built on a promontory jutting out into the loch, the castle had a position of great strategic importance, commanding as it did fine views along the waters, and standing on a major route to the north-east. There are signs that a prehistoric fort was built on the site. Certainly there have been fortifications here from the early thirteenth century. Such an important point would inevitably have become the focus of strife, and such was indeed the case with Urquhart Castle – in the Wars of Independence alone the fortress was taken four times. By the end of the seventeenth century many of the castle's buildings had been destroyed to prevent them falling into the hands of the Jacobites, and the castle had no importance in the Risings of 1715 and 1745. Nevertheless, enough of the structure remains to give an impression of what it must have looked like in its earlier days, and the view from the keep is exceptionally fine.

Many of the rivers and lochs around Loch Ness have been harnessed by the North of Scotland Electricity Board for the production of hydro-electricity, and such is the case at Cannich and along Glen Affric. Once a major route from the west coast at Kintail, Glen Affric today affords passage only to hardy hikers. Despite the effects of hydro-electric developments, little of the beauty of this wild loch has been lost, and it is still possible to tramp the unspoilt tracks along its shores in tranquillity, and to watch the golden eagle soaring high above.

Inverness is the unchallenged capital of the Highlands; from the aptly nicknamed 'Hub of the Highlands' many major routes radiate. Evidence exists that the site has been strategically important for many centuries; indeed, there are signs of prehistoric occupation, with a number of carved stones, vitrified hill forts and burial chambers of some note. By the twelfth century a royal castle

Urquhart Castle on the shore of Loch Ness, Inverness-shire

17

Inverness: in the foreground, the river Ness; in the background the Victorian castle

existed here – Macbeth in fact ruled from Inverness in the eleventh century – and a thriving community became a chartered burgh. The present castle is Victorian, but it is possible that the original castle stood on the same site, for the position is a fine one, perched high above the river.

Little remains in Inverness of any notable age. Queen Mary's House dates back to the sixteenth-century, but is much altered. Abertarff House is probably also sixteenth century; now owned by the National Trust for Scotland, it is leased to An Comunn Gaidhealach (the British Council for Gaeldom). Cromwell left his mark even in this northerly spot. In 1652 his troops built a fortress here – the Citadel – but it was destroyed on the Restoration of Charles II, and all that now remains is the Clock Tower.

An interesting development has been the Eden Court Theatre on the banks of the River Ness. In an imaginative and exhilarating design, the old episcopal Palace of Bishop Eden has been incorporated into the new building, and the complex now hosts many shows and exhibitions. Inverness, despite its history, looks to the future, not to the past, and its importance is as an educational, administrative and marketing centre for the Highlands. Certainly to travellers arriving from the south, Inverness is the door that opens to the north, and to the magnificent mountains and coastline of the west.

The North

North of Inverness the east coast gives little hint of the wild beauty of the hinterland. The Black Isle – not an island at all, but a peninsula – is rich farmland, sheltered and mild. For centuries the Black Isle's towns were favoured trading centres; Fortrose was created a Royal burgh in 1592 and Cromarty, another Royal burgh, has always been an important administrative centre. This was Urquhart land – a family that produced some notable characters, the most remarkable being Sir Thomas Urquhart, translator of Rabelais, who traced his family genealogy, so he claimed, back to Adam. The fine Sir Thomas died in a paroxysm of joyous laughter when he heard of the restoration of Charles II. Another son of the town was the geologist, Hugh Miller. His cottage has been restored by the National Trust for Scotland, and houses a small museum in his memory.

The shores of the Black Isle provide an ideal habitat for waders and wildfowl of many species; Chanonry Point is a favoured migration point, Rosemarkie has a fulmar colony. In spring the pinkfoot goose passes along these shores, and in winter along the Beauly Firth the birdwatcher will spot gooseanders, in summer the Canada goose. Udale Bay on the Cromarty Firth is notable for its ducks and waders, for curlew, godwit and dunlin. On the northern shore at Nigg Bay, wigeon still find peace and plenty among the steel production platforms being manufactured to service the North Sea oil industry.

While the resorts of Speyside became known for their restorative air, and Nairn for its sunny climate and fine beaches, the village of Strathpeffer developed as a spa almost a century earlier. The four sulphur springs and one chalybeate were famous throughout the north of Scotland by the 1770s, although no pump room was built until 1820. A second pump room was added in 1909. Castle Leod, seat of the Earl of Cromartie, stands north of the village.

Many Pictish settlements became the focus for the missionary zeal of evangelical Irish Christians, and there is plentiful evidence of early Christian foundations. St Duthac was born in Tain, and after his death in Ireland his remains were brought back to the town of his birth and his shrine became a place of pilgrimage. James IV made regular visits to the shrine, travelling along the road now known as the King's Causeway to the south of the town. But St Duthac proved less than protective: Robert Bruce's wife, sisters and daughter, seeking sanctuary at this shrine, were seized by the Earl of Ross and handed over to the English. Retribution no doubt followed, for the Earl, wearing St Duthac's coat which was reputed to have magical qualities, was struck down and killed at the Battle of Halidon Hill in 1333. James V, who visited the shrine seven times, died shortly after his last pilgrimage in 1513 – the year of the disastrous Battle of Flodden.

many useful facilities in the town, and every climber descending wearily from the mighty mountain massif comprising Ben Nevis, Aonach Mor, Aonach Beag and Carn Mor Dearg will stumble thankfully into the plentiful bars and restaurants or stock up with fresh provisions for the rucksack.

At Ballachulish the bridge, completed in 1975, replaces the old ferry, obviating the long queues of cars awaiting passage. For those with a destination, timetable and schedules firmly in mind, the bridge is undoubtedly a blessing; but much was lost when the final link was completed. No longer does the traveller sit and contemplate the beauties of Loch Linnhe and Loch Leven, or watch with pleasure the churning foam in the wake of the ferries, or observe their complicated and skilful maneouvering of rock and tide. Time, even in the Highlands, seems more pressing than it used to be.

Beyond Ballachulish, Glencoe runs inland. The rugged peaks of this wild glen are ever evocative of the fearful massacre of 13 February 1692 when many Macdonald clansmen were slain by the Campbell troops who had been billeted on them. Today the magnificent peaks form one of Scotland's most celebrated sporting venues; climbers scale the tremendous pinnacles, and skiers head for the lower slopes at the first hint of snow. The sinister aspect of the glen is not merely one of historical association, however; these mountains are very dangerous, and even experienced mountaineers are killed amid the

At the Pass of Glen Coe; in the background, Aonach Dubh

Buachaille Etive Mór from Rannoch Moor

Opposite:
Glen Etive, Argyll

treacherous peaks. So take care if you intend to scale the slopes – go well prepared and equipped, and tell someone where you are heading.

Beyond these fearsome hills Rannoch Moor stretches away, a huge expanse of bleak and boggy ground. Once the Caledonian Forest grew thick in these parts; now the peat lies 20 feet deep, true wilderness. Uncrossed by road, the intrepid railway breaches the bog, kept 'afloat' in places only by the support of piles of brushwood. This is not man's territory; it belongs to the wild things, the flora that thrive only on bog, to the red deer, the birds of the moor and the golden eagle that soars high above.

The coastal road south from Ballachulish presents a very different aspect, with gentler views and a pretty outlook over Loch Linnhe. Oban is the main focus of this part of the west. Many ferry services operate from here – principally to Mull, Barra, Coll and South Uist – and steamer cruises round the islands are available. But Oban does not just look to the sea; this is a major centre for the Lorn hinterland. Small industries provide Oban with a prosperous economic

foundation – times are not so lean as they were when in 1897 John Stewart McCaig set the local unemployed to work on a project still uncompleted at his death. This, the strange edifice perched on Oban Hill, became known as 'McCaig's Folly', and provides Oban with its best-known landmark.

An even more impressive structure is found not on a hill, but underneath one. Eastwards, beyond Taynuilt and the beautiful shores of Loch Etive, along the impressive Pass of Brander where in 1308 Robert Bruce fought off an ambush by MacDougall clansmen, is Ben Cruachan, a mighty mountain complex comprising seven great peaks. Under all this, burrowed far into the rock, is a vast cavern, like the inside of a cathedral, 300 feet long, 120 high. This remarkable feat of engineering was accomplished for the North of Scotland Hydro-Electricity Board to house mammoth turbo-generators. Cruachan is a pumped storage station, the first that was developed in Scotland. South from here stretches the vast length of Loch Awe. Campbell country this – here that powerful clan built its strongholds. At Kilchurn, at the head of the loch, Colin Campbell of Glenorchy, founder of the Breadalbane branch of the family, held fort in the fifteenth century. To the south, along Glen Aray at Inveraray the Campbell Dukes of Argyll made their seat. The old castle was rebuilt in the eighteenth century, and the village that nestled against its walls was demolished to make room for the planned extensions. The old village may be lost to us, but as a bonus we have the fine burgh planned in its place by Roger Morris and the great William Adam. The castle, despite devastation by fire, houses many treasures as well as displaying fine architectural details such as the Adam chimneypieces within its unique neo-Scottish-baronial exterior.

The waters in this part of Scotland are remarkably rewarding for the fisherman, even in a country famous for fine fish. River Aray behind Inveraray abounds in salmon. Loch Fyne is famous for the exceptionally fine herring, smoked and cured to become 'Loch Fyne kippers', and back up the coast towards Oban, the lochs around Kilmelfort are rich in sea trout. This is delightful countryside, wooded and rolling, with hundreds of sheltered coves to explore and enjoy. The Clachan Bridge – the 'Bridge across the Atlantic' – is a picturesque hump, linking the mainland with Seil island and its neighbouring island of Easdale, famed for its now exhausted slate quarries.

Between Loch Fyne and Loch Long stretches the land mass of Cowal, deeply indented with sea lochs on all sides: Loch Goil, amid the beautiful Argyll Forest Park – a spectacular road along Hell's Glen links Loch Goil with Loch Fyne – the Holy Loch, which has become famous as a US polaris submarine base, Loch Striven and the Kyles of Bute, which separate the island of Bute from this part of the mainland.

Dunoon on Cowal, Rothesay on Bute, these are major resorts on this southerly outpost of the Scottish 'Highlands'. Across the Firth of Clyde lies Glasgow, and to the Glaswegians these ports provide a major escape route from bustling city life. Highlight of the summer season at Dunoon is the Cowal Highland Games, ablaze with the colour of tartan, the air alive with the skirl of the pipes.

The Island of Arran is another major holiday destination. The island has a mild climate and many beautiful glens, and the spectacular peaks of the northern half provide excellent climbing and sweeping vistas to the Hebrides and the

The Isle of Arran: Lamlash,
with Goat Fell behind

Opposite:
The hills of Arran from
Kintyre, Argyll

northern Highlands as well as to the south and Ireland. Across the Kilbrennan Sound to the west the long, south-reaching peninsula comprising Knapdale and Kintyre represents the extreme southerly outpost of the Highlands. Kintyre is connected to Knapdale at Tarbert by a mere one-mile neck of land: Knapdale, in its turn, is severed from the rest of Argyll by the Crinan Canal, cut in 1793-1801. Less important now to the herring fishing boats, it is still much used by yachts and small vessels, a busy, friendly short-cut, with 15 locks, saving a trip round the Mull of Kintyre of some 130 miles.

This south-westerly corner of Scotland was very vulnerable to attack; the first 'Scots' landed here from Ireland in the sixth century, making their seat at Dunadd near Kilmichael Glassary, the controlling centre of their kingdom of Dalriada. As evidence of later threats, buildings such as Castle Sween still survive. This is the oldest stone castle in Scotland, built by Somerled, King of Argyll in the twelfth century, as a base for driving out Norse invaders. There is much evidence of Viking presence in this part of the country; at Tarbert, where

Kintyre joins Knapdale, Magnus Barefoot is said to have dragged his ships across the neck of the isthmus in the eleventh century, thus claiming that Kintyre was an 'island' and under the terms of his treaty, a Norse possession.

It is hardly surprising that the Vikings wished to claim this land as their own; it was fine territory, with exhilarating seascapes and many safe harbours, guaranteed to please these sea-raiders' hearts – and more important, there was a fine rich hinterland for farming and grazing. Kintyre may have changed much since the Vikings were here, but not in essentials. The sea still pounds the western shore and seven tides battle round the Mull of Kintyre; the cattle still get fat and produce fine milk on the lush pasture. From the Mull, Ireland's hills can be clearly seen only 17 miles distant; Muckle Flugga is more than 400 miles to the north. The Mull is south even of Alnwick in England. It is a remarkable corner of the Scottish Highlands.

The Islands

4
Orkney & Shetland

From the southern peninsula of Kintyre to the northerly islands of Orkney and Shetland is a far cry indeed; and if the mainland of Scotland seems diverse in geographical or scenic terms, in history or modern industrial development, the islands around her coast represent not merely one, but hundreds more facets of this fascinating land.

Orkney and Shetland themselves consist not of two, but many islands in two major groups – Orkney alone has 67 – stretching away out into the North Sea. To restore some sense of perspective to map representations usually distorted for convenience: from Muckle Flugga, Shetland's most northerly isle, to South Ronaldsay, Orkney, is roughly the same distance as London to Leeds. And Sumburgh airport on Shetland is over a thousand miles from London – further to the north than Milan is to the south.

These islands, so isolated from the protection of the power centres of Scotland, let alone England, were naturally prey to invaders, and the land-hungry Norsemen, sailing over the waters from Norway, found and conquered them, ruling them as their own.

But Orkney's history can be traced back much earlier than the twelfth century. The great megalithic chambered burial cairn of Maeshowe was the work of neolithic man 4,000 years ago. The precise geometric construction points to a far from primitive people, but the labour involved must have been enormous, however great the skill. This is a tomb for a prince of men. But the treasures that would have lain here in the tomb were pillaged by Viking raiders; and in their place they scratched messages on the walls in their runic characters.

Maeshowe is not Orkney's only prehistoric relic; the Standing Stones of Stenness date from around 1800 BC, and the Bronze Age Ring of Brodgar is the finest henge monument in Scotland. In 1850 a mighty storm blew in from the Atlantic and shifted the dunes around Skara Brae; below, stones belonging to a Stone Age dwelling were revealed, and subsequent excavations have brought to light an entire village, ten houses interconnected by passages and alleyways. Details of domestic life there abounded: fireplaces, stone beds, cupboards, dressers and primitive tools, pointers to the domestic life of this tiny primitive rural community.

In the eighth and ninth centuries AD, the Norsemen swept into these islands, and ruled them with an iron fist until they passed to Scotland in 1468 as part of the dowry of Margaret of Denmark for her marriage with James III. The island earls were powerful, but trouble between them came in 1116 when the joint inheritors of the Jarldom of Orkney, Magnus Erlendson and Hakon Paulson met on Egilsay to settle their differences. The gentle Magnus was slain, and in 1137

The prehistoric standing stones of the Ring of Brodgar, Orkney

the first stone of the cathedral of St Magnus the Martyr was laid in Kirkwall to honour his memory.

The cathedral is truly a splendid building, a fine centrepiece for the island capital. Many other old buildings survive – the twelfth-century Bishop's Palace, and the fine seventeenth-century Earl's Palace, and they provide a tranquil centre for this busy island city. For Orkney, like Shetland, has become a major centre for the oil industry, and the traffic of the oilmen has injected a new economic life into the island.

Yet far from taking over the islands to their detriment, the oil industry has been controlled, contained and channelled to the islanders' benefit. And while mainland Orkney concerns itself with the business of oil, the other islanders, fishermen and crofters, get on with the day to day business of living off the land. Many of the Norse settlers were not merely fighters but also farmers, and their farming legacy lives on in this rich land. But the sea has played its role too, and the safe anchorage of Scapa Flow was used as a naval base from 1912. After the erection of the Churchill Barriers in 1939, the base was thought to be impregnable.

The island of Flotta protects Scapa Flow at its southern end. Now it has another importance, as a major oil terminal for crude oil from the Piper Field.

Stromness, Orkney's former capital

The Orcadians have taken care to preserve the home industries of crofting and fishing; and they take pride in the richness and variety of the bird life on their islands. Three reserves on Orkney are managed by the Royal Society for the Protection of Birds. The little island of Copinsay, with its fine cliffs, is one of these, and has large nesting colonies notably of kittiwake and guillemot. Take your binoculars wherever you travel on these northerly isles, for your rewards may be rich; auks and skuas, Arctic terns, phalaropes, shearwaters, and waders and divers in their hundreds may be observed at leisure amid this splendid coastal scenery. Some of the rock formations that fringe Orkney's coastline are indeed spectacular. The island of Hoy, Orkney's second largest, boasts some of the finest scenery, with Britain's highest perpendicular cliff – a dizzying 1,140 feet vertically down into the sea – and the famous Old Man of Hoy, a column of red sandstone on a tiny promontory, rising sheer to 450 feet.

Midway between Orkney and Shetland lies the tiny island of Fair Isle, which has become renowned world-wide among ornithologists. From the Bird

Observatory set up in 1948, studies have been made of migrating birds which use the tiny island as a staging post, and more than 300 species have been observed. Fair Isle has achieved lasting fame, too, from the intricate and colourful knitting traditionally worked by the womenfolk.

More than 100 miles from the Scottish mainland lies the Shetland archipelago, a vast and complex pattern of islands – 100 in all. The coastline convolutes in great jagged contortions for more than 3,000 miles, striking again and again into the fragile land-mass in great 'voes' or sea-lochs. Remote the islands may be, but they were undoubtedly occupied by prehistoric man; the excavations at Jarlshof on the south of Shetland have revealed houses dating back to 2000 BC. Bronze and Iron Age settlers also made their homes here, and more than 60 neolithic sites have been uncovered elsewhere in these islands.

Sea-locked as the islanders were, their defences also had to look to the sea, and evidence of these defences is abundant. There are 95 brochs in Shetland – remarkable buildings that housed the local community in emergency. The

St Magnus Bay, Shetland

windowless walls, 'waisted' rather like an egg-timer to provide an unscalable overhang, would have risen to some 50 feet, with a series of galleries within to provide access to the top of the tower. The courtyard would have housed the neighbouring community and their livestock. The best-preserved example of such a broch is at Mousa, still standing 43 feet high. The monks of St Ninian's were perhaps less well protected, for treasure, hastily buried by them at first sight of Norse marauders, was discovered on St Ninian's Isle – brooches, a communion spoon, silver bowls of exquisite craftsmanship.

Shetland's 'treasure trove' now is undoubtedly the economic boom occasioned by its proximity to North Sea oilfields. From a remote little airport designed to service these distant isles, Sumburgh has become one of the busiest airports in Scotland; and Lerwick, the island's capital, is now a truly cosmopolitan town, humming with activity. Lerwick was always a busy fishing village, but it did not develop as the island's capital until the early nineteenth century. The old town huddles together, the strong grey stone houses built end-

Lerwick, Shetland's capital city

on to the prevailing winds blowing in from the sea. But while it is largely the oil-related developments that have forced Lerwick to expand into suburbia, fishing still plays an important part in the town's economy, and the fine harbour gives shelter not just to Shetland's vessels, but to the many trawlers that sail these northern seas.

For many islanders fishing provides employment, and the trawlers set out daily in their quest for cod and herring, haddock and whiting. Lobster and crab are caught locally, too, and more jobs are provided by the fish freezing and processing plants around the environs of the harbour.

Fair Isle is famed for its brightly-coloured, highly patterned knitted garments; in Shetland the tradition of knitting is different. Here the speciality is fine work – so fine that a Shetland shawl was tested for quality by pulling it through a wedding ring. Such work is rare in these days of the knitting machine, but the persistent seeker may still have a lucky find. The quality of the wool is, of course, critical to results, and Shetland produces fine wool in plenty for sheep-farming is important to the island's economy. The gourmet should seek out a dish of Shetland lamb, for this meat is fine, delicate and highly prized.

Sheep are not Shetland's only livestock, and while herds of ponies no longer run wild on the islands, these tiny, hardy and captivating animals do roam free in many parts. The birdlife, too, as on Orkney and Fair Isle, is remarkable, and many areas are protected. Fetlar boasts the nesting place of the snowy owl, and while access is strictly limited, especially during the nesting season, the visitor unable to spot this magnificent bird will not be disappointed by his visit to the islands, for there is much besides to observe.

Despite all the modern developments that Shetland has learnt to accommodate, to live in these islands is to learn to live with the elements, with the sea and with the wind. The ties with Scandinavia are strong – as strong, almost, as those with Scotland; and in lasting remembrance of their Norse ancestry, the Shetlanders annually celebrate the coming of Spring with the 'Up-Helly-Aa' festival, a quite recent innovation in which they ceremonially burn a brightly-painted 30-foot longship to welcome the return of the sun after the endless night of winter.

5
The Outer Hebrides

From the Atlantic the wind howls in, unbroken and unabated over the ragged coastline, the jumbled islets of the 'Long Isle'. Clouds, laden with water, are blown straight across these low islands, to drop their rain elsewhere, on the hills of the Highlands; but the wind gusts here in gale force with monotonous regularity. At Barra Head it has been known to move a 42-ton rock five feet from its site, and to blow small fish straight up a 600-foot cliff to land on the grass at the top – ready-delivered supper for the man bold enough to retrieve them!

The wind and the sea have between them shaped the Hebrides. Pounding for centuries on the coastline of the western shores, they have created the sands – vast stretches, mile upon mile, unbroken, unlittered, unpeopled. Sunny these beaches may be, but the relentless winds guarantee their quiet. Behind the marram dunes that prevent the sand from enroaching on the hinterland lies the glorious machair, meadows of flowers as far as the eye can see – daisy, buttercup, clover, thyme, pansy, and dozens more. On this pasture the island cattle graze, and their milk is witness to its scented sweetness.

The machair is surely the crowning glory of the Outer Hebrides; inland lies bleak moorland, in places tolerable grazing land, elsewhere black peat bog, providing a source of fuel, but little else.

Crofters and fishermen people these isles, making best use of the sheltered harbours on the eastern shores, the rich marram on the west. In Harris and Lewis homesteads were traditionally 'black houses': long, low buildings with double stone walls some nine feet thick, filled with brushwood and peat – surely the earliest cavity insulation – and with a thatched roof stoutly pegged on the inner of the walls to prevent it being lifted by the wind. A hole in the ceiling sufficed for ventilation and light, and the smell of the peat fire filled the building and hung on the air. Today the island people prefer modern conveniences and build themselves grand new houses next to the old, but few new buildings are as stout or as cosy as the old 'black house'. Next to the house stands the peat stack, the winter's fuel supply, laid in during the summer months. Peat is a major commodity, particularly on Lewis's famous Black Moor, 10,000 acres of brown peat bog, liberally sprinkled with freshwater lochs.

Few islanders rely on crofting for their livelihood; fishing, building, road-making are all important industries, and on Harris and Lewis the cottage industry of weaving plays an important part. In an age when cheap man-made fibres are widely available, the dearer, labour-intensive Harris tweed has a smaller share of the textile market than it once had. But nothing compares with the fine quality of the hand-woven wool, and Harris tweed is still highly prized the world over.

Overleaf:
Barra: the beach near
Eoligarry

Stornoway is the busy capital of the Western Isles. Now its administrative centre, it hosts the ferry terminal and airport, boasts a fine and well-used harbour, and has even become caught up in the North Sea oil industry with the building of platforms and barges at nearby Arnish Point. Barra, too, boasts an airport – the only airport in the world to be washed clean by the sea twice a day.

Not one but hundreds of islands make up the Long Isle, and despite their proximity they have little in common. Lewis has its rocky shores and vast Black Moor, Harris its hills and sweeping beaches; North Uist, particularly ravaged by glacial activity, is almost more water than land, while South Uist has fine land for crofting. Yet one thing binds these islands together – their strong Gaelic heritage.

The inheritance of the islands, of course, is Norse; but long before the Vikings landed their longboats on these shores, Neolithic man settled here, and the evidence of his occupation is plentiful. There are many monoliths and chambered cairns, and at Callanish in West Lewis is one of the most impressive stone henges in Britain. The mighty stones have stood sentinel for 4,000 years on this windswept site, mysterious survivors of the ravages of time and weather. A chambered cairn indicates a grave, the cruciform pattern hints at a form of sun-worship; and it may be that these stones, and the network of monoliths on these islands, were also used for complicated calculations of time and season.

The Picts, whose language was a form of Gaelic, also left evidence of their presence. Vitrified forts, whose walls were cemented by burning peat, kelp seaweed and wood, are more common on the mainland, but defensive walled enclosures – duns – are very plentiful in the Hebrides. A more sophisticated building was the broch – Mousa on Shetland is the finest surviving example, but Dun Carloway on Lewis stands over 30 feet high. These brochs were probably built as defences against early Viking raiders.

Defences could do little against the power of the marauding Norsemen, and by AD 850 the Hebrides had fallen to their might – so much so that the islands were called by the Scots *Innisgal*, 'islands of foreigners'. Yet their legacy in the Outer Hebrides is not a tangible one – not even a stone building survives. Place names reveal much of their society and their ways though, and even the island of Harris derives its name from the Norse *Hérsir*, Administrator.

In 1156 Somerled the Great, Norse by ancestry, Scots in his loyalties, seized power in the isles, and with his rule began a long and peaceful episode in the islands' history. Under the rule of the Lords of the Isles, the Hebrides took their own course, quite separate from that of mainland Scotland, laying down the vast Celtic heritage that the islands draw on, even today. The clan system prevailed here until the final defeat of Charles Edward Stuart at Culloden in 1746. With the Acts of Parliament of 1747 the powers of heritable jurisdiction of the chiefs was effectively removed – but the chiefs, long used to power, imposed their own form of economic feudalism. Combined with years of poor harvests, life became too harsh for the islanders, and they began to emigrate in their thousands to the American colonies, the beginning of a tide that was not to end until the 1860s.

The tenacity with which the islanders hold to their land is a tribute to the rugged determination of their character. Even the small population of outlying St Kilda, 50 miles west of Harris in the Atlantic Ocean, eked out a living from the infertile land until as recently as 1930. Now this island group is visited only by

naturalists, who come to observe the distinctive species that have evolved here, the St Kilda wren and mouse, and the Soay sheep, and to watch the vast colonies of gannets and other seabirds that nest around the dramatic cliffs.

South Harris: Seilebost Bay, with the hills of North Harris behind

If the intrepid traveller ventures as far as St Kilda, few even of the most determined visitors to the Western Isles will visit the westernmost point of Scotland – Rockall, a barren rock almost 200 miles west of St Kilda, far out into the Atlantic Ocean. The rock was legally incorporated into the United Kingdom, in 'that part known as Scotland' on 10 February 1972 – in fact, it became a part of Harris. The rock holds no interest to the visitor, but it may play a key role in the extension of Britain's fishing and mineral rights.

St Kilda and Rockall are far-flung even in these strung-out islands, and few of the main group are inaccessible. A system of car ferries and causeways links the main islands, and exploration is no longer a major task. Barra, with its satellites the most southerly island of the group, may be reached from mainland Scotland by air; and there can be no finer approach to these islands on a clear day than the low sweep in across sapphire seas and silver sands to this strangest of airports. From Barra's hills – low by mainland standards – the views are nevertheless excellent, across the wide expanse of sea to Skye, Rhum and Eigg, and due east to the mainland at Knoydart and Ardnamurchan.

Kisimul Castle, a fine example of a stone-built Norman castle, stands impressively in Castlebay, for centuries a stronghold of the MacNeils of Barra. The stout fortifications of the castle were well utilized in the early seventeenth century by a former chief who used the castle to store his booty after piratical raids on Ireland and on the passing ships of other nations. Queen Elizabeth of England, annoyed by the repeated disappearance of her ships in these waters, demanded of James VI of Scotland that the pirate chief be brought to trial. MacNeil, lured to Edinburgh by a ruse, had the wit and presence of mind to remind James that it was Elizabeth who had executed Mary, Queen of Scots, his mother, and he was allowed to walk free. The castle was restored between 1938 and 1959 by the 45th chief.

On South Uist Bonnie Prince Charlie sought refuge while awaiting transport to France. Life, it seems, was not all misery for the defeated Prince, for a visitor told of a fine meal of 'a half stone of butter laid on a timber plate, and near a leg of beef laid on a chest before us' – followed by a true Highland drinking session lasting three days and nights. The Prince had a harder head than any – a sad foretaste, perhaps, of his later alcoholic degeneracy in the capitals of Europe. On Benbecula, between North and South Uist, the Prince met Flora Macdonald and finally escaped to Skye, dressed as her maid.

North Uist, with its rich endowment of fresh and seawater lochs, is an angler's paradise; birdwatchers will revel in the unparalleled wetland reserve at Balranald, home of the rare red-necked phalarope; and for the botanist the fertile machair on the west provides splendid examples of many species of wild flowers.

Eight miles across the water to the north, Harris and Lewis loom large. At Rodel on the southernmost tip of Harris is the charming sixteenth-century St Clement's Church, burial place of the Macleods. Just to the north is Leverburgh, whose name is perhaps the most lasting memorial to the substantial effort and financial investment of Lord Leverhulme to transform the little village into a

55

The village of Northton, South Harris

major port and to provide much-needed employment. After his death in 1924, the improvement plans were abandoned.

Harris's capital is Tarbert, ferry terminal and the best centre for exploring the island. Stroll along the shores of Loch Laxdale on a bright summer's evening and watch the salmon jump in the cool green loch; the Mediterranean for all its blueness could never rival the translucent clarity of these waters, nor the scented warmth of the south match the sharp cleanness of the air of Harris.

To cross the hills that divide Harris from Lewis is to enter a different country. Flatter land this, moor-covered and boggy, and with a scattered crofting community round the coastal reaches. Here, as in Harris, the crofters work a system of 'lazy-beds' to provide cultivable, well-drained soil. Strips between three and eight feet wide are built up like platforms by digging trenches between and piling soil up on to the beds. Layers of seaweed are used to improve the richness of the soil.

A journey across the backbone of Lewis, across the wide reaches of loch and moor, round the north western shore, past places far, far more ancient than recorded history, terminates in the wild, exposed Butt of Lewis. From here to the west and the north, there is nothing but the sea.

To the islanders, sea and loch are an immutable part of everyday living, to be respected and wherever possible used to advantage. But to the summer visitor these waters play a different role. The Atlantic breakers, rolling in over the vast stretches of sand, their translucent green subtly changing to blue and back to green, put the bustle of city life into a new perspective; and the lochans, so patched across the moorland that they seem merely held together by wisps of reed and tufts of grass, reflect the immensity of sky and cloud, conjoining the elements in a glorious fusion of shimmering light.

6

The Inner Hebrides

Across the waters of the Minch from the 'Long Isle' lies that most wildly beautiful, most romanticized island of Scotland – Skye; and it would have been from this direction that the Norse invaders came in their longboats when they dubbed the place Skúyo, Cloud Island, because of the cloud-capped peaks of the Cuillin mountains. The Norsemen ruled not only Orkney and Shetland and the Outer Hebrides, but the islands that hug the west coast of Scotland also; and the signs of their presence are everywhere. From Dun Sgathaich on Sleat in the most southerly part of Skye they ruled the Hebrides, and this fort, with its fine views of the Cuillins, was one of the most important centres of power in the west. The fort passed into the hands of the Macleods, then to the Macdonalds. Between them these two clans held power in Skye for centuries, the Macdonalds based in the south at Armadale, the Macleods in the north from their impressive stronghold of Dunvegan.

When Bonnie Prince Charlie was hunted across the length and breadth of Scotland after his defeat at Culloden in 1746, it was to Skye that his flight took him after his sojourn in the Outer Isles. This episode in the young Prince's life has perhaps more than any other become fabled almost out of recognition; yet whose sense of the romantic could resist the tale of the charming young prince, disguised as the serving woman of his brave and loyal clanswoman, Flora Macdonald, escaping from under the very noses of the Hanoverian troops searching for him. Largely through Flora's courage the Prince made good his escape to France. Flora herself, like so many thousands of her kin, emigrated to the New World to escape the hardships of life in the Old.

The romantic element in Skye's history has perhaps coloured the impressions of poets and artists through the centuries. Scott's *Lord of the Isles,* in the best tradition of Regency romanticism, portrays Loch Coruisk at the heart of the Cuillin hills as a place of gloomy magnificence. And many were the artists who, influenced by his portrayal, depicted the loch with an overwhelmingly dismal aspect.

The climbers of today know this land in another light; and climbers there are in plenty, for the Cuillins provide some of the best climbing in Britain. Few of Skye's summits can be achieved without rock-climbing, but Sgurr Alasdair, the highest in Skye, may be ascended from the campsite at Glen Brittle via Coire Lagain. The dreary scree-covered approach provides little relief for a thousand feet or more, but the rewards at the summit are manifold, for this is one of the finest viewpoints in the Highlands.

Portree is Skye's capital; 'Port Righ' – 'King's Haven' – was so named in 1540 after the visit of James V in an attempt to reconcile feuding Macdonald and

Skye: The Cuillins seen across Loch Slapin from Torrin

Macleod clansmen, and to exert his authority over the more remote parts of his kingdom. The harbour, protected by the island of Raasay just offshore, is a good one, and well used despite the deceptive aura of prettiness. To the north, on Trotternish, stand the Quiraing and the Old Man of Storr, a series of fantastic rocky pinnacles. The Old Man of Storr stands 160 feet high, a startling monolith perched precariously on the rim of a corrie. The Quiraing is a natural fortress, and amid its castellated spires raiders once hid their stolen cattle. This rocky eastern shore bears no resemblance to the western coast of Trotternish which is rich land, and well crofted. From Uig Bay, its wide green arms outspread to welcome the sea, a ferry sails to the Western Isles.

Across Loch Snizort, at the head of Loch Dunvegan, stands Dunvegan Castle, ancient seat of the chiefs of the Clan Leod. For over 700 years the Macleods have held this land as their territory, and before them, in the ninth century, the Norsemen fortified this spot also. This present building dates back at least as far as the fifteenth century, and the stout fortifications are testimony of the necessity of good defence in years long gone, A moat is the outermost defence, and some of the walls of the castle are ten feet thick. Myth and legend are indistinguishable from history where these redoubtable chiefs are concerned. Rory Mor, 13th chief of the Macleods, left for posterity his famous drinking horn, which held five pints of claret. A new chief was required to drain the horn in a single draught! The castle also houses the 'Fairy Flag' which, it is said, brings victory to the Macleods in battle. The flag is thought to have been captured from the Saracens during one of the Crusades, and on the two occasions it has been shown in battle, victory has followed.

The loyalty of the Clan Leod, whose adherents are now spread world-wide, was re-kindled by the inspired leadership of the late Dame Flora MacLeod, and the castle is now visited and inspected with pride by many thousands of visitors and followers of the Clan. For the clansman from Toronto or Sydney, Cape Town or Atlanta, these walls are symbols of generations of kinship, loosened perhaps but not severed, and the mountains of Skye provide for them an incomparable setting.

To the south of Skye lies a small collection of islands, whose anglicized names sound strange indeed; Rhum, Muck, Eigg and Canna. Rhum is the largest of these islands, rising gloriously out of the sea, its three massive peaks visible for many miles. Like most of the west of Scotland, Rhum suffered irreparable depopulation in the mid-eighteenth century, and the introduction of large numbers of red deer completed the damage to the land. After the acquisition of the island in 1957 by the Nature Conservancy, the wildlife situation was brought under a measure of control, and under strict supervision visits are now permitted for the study of the island's geology and botany. A recent and successful experiment conducted from Rhum has been the re-introduction to Scotland of the rare white sea-eagle as a nesting species.

The island of Mull, the largest of the Inner Hebrides, may lack the fierce grandeur of the mountain ranges of Skye, but the deficiency is more than compensated for by scenic variety ranging from wild moorland to silvery sands by way of lush vegetation and dramatic cliff formations. Tobermory at the north of the island is its capital, and a fitting one. Round the sheltered harbour the brightly painted houses cluster, and steamers, fishing vessels and gay dinghies come and go. In the bay lies Tobermory's hidden treasure: a Spanish galleon, seeking shelter after the defeat of the Armada in 1588, was blown up and sank without trace, and with it sank a treasure store of some 30,000 Spanish ducats. Silt in the bay has to date made recovery of the treasure impossible.

From Tobermory to Craignure and the ancient Maclean stronghold, Duart Castle, the roads are good and fast, for Craignure is the main ferry destination from Oban, and in addition to transporting local and visiting traffic to and from the island, the summer ferries set down thousands of visitors bent on a coach trip around the island or a pilgrimage to the island of Iona. Duart Castle commands the seaward approach to the island, and has occupied this fine

Overleaf left:
Mull: the Inner Isles steamer at Tobermory pier

Overleaf right:
Mull: Duart Castle on its crag above the Sound of Mull

59

Mull: Snow-covered Ben More above Glen More

strategic position since the thirteenth century. This is the seat of the Macleans, their stronghold until 1691 when the castle was forfeited by William of Orange. It fell into disrepair, and was restored early this century. On a fine day, the view from the battlements can extend to some 40-odd miles, across the Firth of Lorne to the mighty summit of Ben Nevis.

Beyond Duart the road, built to cope with the heavy flow of traffic to Iona, runs past Loch Spelve where the Macleans anchored their war galleys – the old slipways are still visible. A minor road runs south to Loch Buie, the so-called 'Garden of Mull', sheltered, fertile land. Here the other branch of the Macleans of Mull, the Maclaines of Lochbuie, had their own stronghold, Moy Castle. Five miles round the coast – a rough walk – is the tiny sheltered Carsaig Bay (accessible by road from Pennyghael). Warmed by the sun on the south-facing rocks, the brambles here in autumn grow as big as loganberries; and on a summer's evening the peaceful lapping of the waves on the stone jetty is disturbed only by the sound of a diver's haunting call. Across the golden waters as the sun sinks to the west, the Paps of Jura rise, triple peaks, purple against the light.

Iona Abbey, founded by St Patrick in the sixth century, on the isle of Iona

Round the western reaches of the island, the roads are very different. Here the single-track road meanders up hill and down dale, providing ever-changing vistas for the enjoyment of the traveller. At Calgary silver sands slope gently under the lapping waves; beyond, a profusion of crimson fuchsia hangs heavy on the roadside hedges. By Loch na Keal rocky beaches hide a wealth of oysters and mussels for those who have the time to search for them; and across the waters towers Mull's mountain, Ben More. Beyond the Ben the road runs under the treacherous Gribun Cliffs, rising sheer from the sea; hold your breath as you pass by – their menacing aspect is no empty threat, and the cliffs could all too easily become a rolling rockslide. Inland across the moors the road turns. Cast your eyes skywards for a glimpse of buzzard or golden eagle. On round Loch Scridain where the salmon virtually beg to be caught, past the cluster of cottages at Pennyghael, through Bunessan and across the bleak and exposed Ross of Mull, the road ends at Fionnphort. Here lies one of Mull's most famous offshore islands, Iona. In AD 563 St Columba landed here from Ireland, bringing with him his evangelical Christian message. Despite repeated destruction by invaders, the Christian community in this tiny island has always survived. Iona has for many centuries been regarded as a place of great holiness, and here were brought for burial the Kings of Scotland and of Ireland, and of Norway also.

Clear across the sea on a cloudless day can be seen Staffa, Mull's other satellite island of great note. Staffa's curious construction of basaltic pillars and vast caverns have made it for centuries a place to be visited and marvelled over. Scott, Wordsworth, Tennyson, Keats, all came and inspected the towering Fingal's Cave, and Mendelssohn was moved by its magnificent dimensions and the rushing echoes of the sea to compose his 'Hebrides' overture, also called 'Fingal's Cave'.

Beyond Staffa lie the Treshnish Isles, a curiously assorted group of islands rich in birdlife and a breeding place of the grey seal. The Manx shearwater nests on these isles, and flocks of this beautiful bird may be passed on the approach to the islands. Puffins, cheerful little birds with their comical bright bills, hurry to and fro, and gannets, with a wingspan as mighty as the eagle's plummet spectacularly into the sea from great heights. This is their territory, and man is but a privileged witness to their activities. Past the Treshnish Isles, Coll and Tiree spread long and low, welcome hosts to the sailor bound for the Outer Hebrides.

Islay is the southernmost island of the Inner Hebrides. The name, *Ila*, means bent like a bow, an apt description of the island's curved appearance. At its heart lies Loch Finlaggan, where the Macdonald Lords of the Isles held their council in the fourteenth and fifteenth centuries. Eilean Mor still bears the ruins of a castle which was once a place of considerable size; and nearby lies the tiny Council Isle where 14 island chiefs rallied to advise their Lord.

Bowmore is now the island's capital. Killarrow Parish Church by the village is a curious round structure – built without corners, it is said, so that the devil might have no place to hide. Port Ellen is one of the island's main ports, and nearby are some of Islay's most famous distilleries – Ardbeg, Lagavulin, Laphraig. These fine malt whiskies have a peaty aroma; like all good Scotch whiskies they depend for their distinctive qualities not merely on carefully controlled technology, but on the inimitable combination of the air and water on the island.

Port Askaig is Islay's other main port, with ferry connections to Kintyre and to Jura. The unmistakable triple peaks of this island are known as the Paps of Jura. The island's single road terminates some nine miles south of the most northern tip of the island. From this point may be seen Corryvreckan, a whirlpool notorious amongst all seagoers. The tides, punching relentlessly against each other between the narrow gap between Scarba and Jura, create a swirling pool that no man enters save at his peril.

West of Jura lie Colonsay and Oronsay, small, fertile islands linked at low tide. Colonsay House has a splendid Hebridean sub-tropical garden, and the mild climate and uninterrupted calm of these islands make them an excellent destination for the peace-loving visitor.

The islands of Western Scotland number in hundreds, and the excitement of discovering them for yourself cannot be captured within the pages of a book. With the echoes of W. H. Murray's words in your ears go, then, and see them for yourself:

On a cloudless morning of early June, 1936, I climbed on to the summit of Sgurr Alasdair in the Cuillin of Skye, and for the first time saw the Hebrides whole, as an archipelago fringing the North Atlantic....At that time of year Scotland's west seaboard has a peculiar clarity of atmosphere....By a trick of light the sea appeared to slope down from the horizon, in a flat calm so very like polished ice that I imagined the isles like curling stones about to slide into the mainland. Their fabled mystery, which they commonly owe to haze or light cloud, was no less marked in that crystal air, for their edge of the ocean site was made so plain. A realm of several hundred islands lay awaiting discovery....